Reversible Ripple
Afghans™

Contents

Brocade Ripple

Brocade Ripple

SKILL LEVEL

EASY

FINISHED SIZE
46 x 53 inches

MATERIALS
- Caron Simply Soft Collection medium (worsted) weight yarn (6 oz/315 yds/170g per skein):
  5 skeins #0010 cypress (A)
- Caron Simply Soft medium (worsted) weight yarn (6 oz/315 yds/170g per skein):
  4 skeins #9703 bone (B)
- Size I/9/5.5mm crochet hook or size needed to obtain gauge

GAUGE
4 sc = 1¼ inches; 12 sc rows = 4 inches

PATTERN NOTES
Weave in loose ends as work progresses.

Change colors *(see Stitch Guide)* in last stitch at end of indicated row.

Carry unused color along edge of work.

When working finishing trim, make sure to work over the unused yarn that has been carried along the side.

SPECIAL STITCH
Front post treble crochet-single crochet (fptr-sc): Leaving last lp on hook, **fptr** *(see Stitch Guide)* around indicated st. Leaving last lp on hook, sc in st directly behind fptr just made *(3 lps on hook)*, yo, draw lp through 3 lps on hook.

AFGHAN
BODY
Row 1 (RS): With A, ch 208, sc in 2nd ch from hook, sc in each of next 3 chs, *3 sc in next ch, sc in each of next 4 chs, sk next 2 chs, sc in each of next 4 chs, rep from * across to last 5 chs, 3 sc in next ch, sc in each of next 4 chs, turn.

Row 2: Ch 1, **sc dec** *(see Stitch Guide)* in first 2 sc, sc in each of next 3 sc, *3 sc in next sc, sc in each of next 4 sc, sk next 2 sc, sc in each of next 4 sc, rep from * across to last 6 sc, 3 sc in next sc, sc in each of next 3 sc, **change color** *(see Pattern Notes)* to B in last st, sc dec in last 2 sc, drop A, **do not fasten off**, turn.

Rows 3 & 4: Rep row 2. At end of row 4, change color to A in last sc, drop B, do not fasten off, turn.

Row 5: Ch 1, sc dec in first 2 sc, sc in each of next 3 sc, *sc in next sc, **fptr-sc** *(see Special Stitch)* around 2nd sc of next 3-sc group 3 rows below, sc in same sc as previous 2 sc on working row, sc in each of next 4 sc, sk next 2 sc, sc in each of next 4 sc, rep from * across to last 6 sc, sc in next sc, fptr-sc around 2nd sc of next 3-sc group 3 rows below, sc in same sc as previous 2 sc on working row, sc in each of next 3 sc, sc dec in last 2 sc, turn.

Row 6: Rep row 2, change color to B at end of row, drop A, do not fasten off, turn.

Rows 7 & 8: Rep row 2. At end of row 8, change color to A, drop B, do not fasten off, turn.

Row 9: Ch 1, sc dec in first 2 sc, sc in next sc, fptr-sc around next tr 3 rows below, sc in next sc on working row, *3 sc in next sc, sc in next sc, fptr-sc around same tr 3 rows below, sc in each of next 2 sc on working row, sk next 2 sc, sc in each of next 2 sc, fptr-sc around next tr 3 rows below, sc in next sc on working row, rep from * across to last 6 sc, 3 sc in next sc, sc in next sc, fptr-sc around same tr 3 rows below, sc in next sc on working row, sc dec in last 2 sc, turn.

Row 10: Rep row 2, change color to B at end of row, drop A, do not fasten off, turn.

Rows 11 & 12: Rep row 2. At end of row 12, change color to A, drop B, do not fasten off, turn.

Row 13: Ch 1, sc dec in first 2 sc, fptr-sc around next tr 3 rows below, sc in each of next 2 sc on working row, *3 sc in next sc, sc in each of next 2 sc, fptr-sc around next tr 3 rows below, sc in next sc on working row, sk next 2 sc, sc in next sc, fptr-sc around next tr 3 rows below, sc in each of next 2 sc on working row, rep from * across to last 6 sc, 3 sc in next sc, sc in each of next 2 sc, fptr-sc around next tr 3 rows below, sc dec in last 2 sc on working row, turn.

Row 14: Rep row 2, change color to B at end of row, drop A, do not fasten off, turn.

Rows 15 & 16: Rep row 2. At end of row 16, change color to A, drop B, do not fasten off, turn.

Rows 17–148: [Rep rows 5–16 consecutively] 11 times.

Rows 149–158: Rep rows 5–14. At end of row 158, fasten off B, do not fasten off A, turn to work down one long side of afghan.

FIRST SIDE EDGING
Row 1 (WS): With WS of Afghan facing, ch 1, working in ends of rows, sc evenly spaced across long edge of Afghan, turn.

Row 2: Ch 1, sc in each sc across. Fasten off.

2ND SIDE EDGING
Row 1 (WS): With WS of Afghan facing, working in ends of rows on rem long side of Afghan, join A with sl st in end of row, ch 1, sc evenly spaced across long edge of Afghan, turn.

Row 2: Ch 1, sc in each sc across. Fasten off. ■

Vanilla Cream
Ripple

SKILL LEVEL

EASY

FINISHED SIZE
54 x 56 inches

MATERIALS
- Caron Simply Soft medium
  (worsted) weight yarn (6 oz/
  315 yds/170g per skein):
  - 7 skeins #9703 bone *(A)*
  - 3 skeins #9742 grey heather *(B)*
- Caron Simply Soft Collection medium
  (worsted) weight yarn (6 oz/315 yds/170g
  per skein):
  - 3 skeins #0001 vanilla *(C)*
- Size I/9/5.5mm crochet hook
  or size needed to obtain gauge

GAUGE
4 sc = 1¼ inches; 13 rows = 4 inches

PATTERN NOTES
Weave in loose ends as work progresses.

Change colors *(see Stitch Guide)* in last stitch at
end of indicated row.

Carry unused color along edge of work.

When working finishing trim, make sure to work
over the unused yarn that has been carried
along the side.

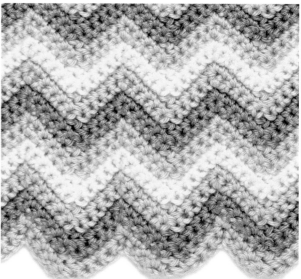

SPECIAL STITCH
**Front post treble crochet cluster-single crochet (fptr
cl-sc):** Leaving last lp of each st on hook, **fptr**
(see Stitch Guide) twice around indicated st,
yo, pull through 2 lps on hook *(2 lps on hook)*.
Leaving last lp on hook, sc in st directly behind
fptr cl just made *(3 lps on hook)*, yo, draw lp
through 3 lps on hook.

AFGHAN
BODY

Row 1 (RS): With A, ch 241, sc in 2nd ch from hook, sc in each of next 3 chs, *3 sc in next ch, sc in each of next 4 chs, sk next 2 chs, sc in each of next 4 chs, rep from * across to last 5 chs, 3 sc in next ch, sc in each of next 4 chs, turn.

Row 2: Ch 1, **sc dec** (*see Stitch Guide*) in first 2 sc, sc in each of next 3 sc, *3 sc in next sc, sc in each of next 4 sc, sk next 2 sc, sc in each of next 4 sc, rep from * across to last 6 sc, 3 sc in next sc, sc in each of next 3 sc, **change color** (*see Pattern Notes*) to B in last st, sc dec in last 2 sc, drop A, **do not fasten off**, turn.

Rows 3 & 4: Rep row 2. At end of row 4, change color to A, drop B, do not fasten off, turn.

Row 5: Ch 1, sc dec in first 2 sc, sc in each of next 3 sc, *sc in next sc, **fptr cl-sc** (*see Special Stitch*) around 2nd sc of next 3-sc group 4 rows below, sc in same sc as previous 2 sc on working row, sc in each of next 4 sc, sk next 2 sc, sc in each of next 4 sc, rep from * across to last 6 sc, sc in next sc, fptr cl-sc around 2nd sc of next 3-sc group 4 rows below, sc in same sc as previous 2 sc on working row, sc in each of next 3 sc, sc dec in last 2 sc, turn.

Row 6: Rep row 2, change color to C at end of row, drop A, do not fasten off, turn.

Rows 7 & 8: Rep row 2. At end of row 8, change color to A, drop C, do not fasten off, turn.

Row 9: Ch 1, sc dec in first 2 sc, sc in each of next 3 sc, *sc in next sc, fptr cl-sc around 2nd sc of next 3-sc group 4 rows below, sc in same sc as previous 2 sc on working row, sc in each of next 4 sc, sk next 2 sc, sc in each of next 4 sc, rep from * across to last 6 sc, sc in next sc, fptr cl-sc around 2nd sc of next 3-sc group 4 rows below, sc in same sc as previous 2 sc on working row, sc in each of next 3 sc, sc dec in last 2 sc, turn.

Row 10: Rep row 2, change color to B at end of row, drop A, do not fasten off, turn.

Rows 11 & 12: Rep row 2. At end of row 12, change color to A, drop B, do not fasten off, turn.

Rows 13 & 14: Rep rows 9 and 10. At end of row 14, change color to C, drop A, do not fasten off, turn.

Rows 15–182: [Rep rows 7–14 consecutively] 21 times. At end of row 182, fasten off B and C, do not fasten off A, turn to work down one long side of afghan.

FIRST SIDE EDGING

Row 1 (WS): With WS of Afghan facing, ch 1, working in ends of rows, sc evenly spaced across long edge of Afghan, turn.

Row 2: Ch 1, sc in each sc across. Fasten off.

2ND SIDE EDGING

Row 1 (WS): With WS of Afghan facing, working in ends of rows on rem long side of Afghan, join A with sl st in end of row, ch 1, sc evenly spaced across long edge of Afghan, turn.

Row 2: Ch 1, sc in each sc across. Fasten off. ■

Sweetheart Ripple

Sweetheart Ripple

SKILL LEVEL

EASY

FINISHED SIZE
48 x 62 inches

MATERIALS
- Caron Simply Soft medium (worsted) weight yarn (6 oz/ 315 yds/170g per skein):
  - 5 skeins #9722 plum wine *(A)*
  - 4 skeins #9730 autumn red *(B)*
- Size I/9/5.5mm crochet hook or size needed to obtain gauge

4 MEDIUM

GAUGE
5 sc = 1½ inches; 12 sc rows = 4 inches

PATTERN NOTES
Weave in loose ends as work progresses.

Change colors *(see Stitch Guide)* in last stitch at end of indicated row.

Carry unused color along edge of afghan.

When working finishing trim, make sure to work over the unused yarn that has been carried along the side.

Heart pattern in afghan is visible when afghan is turned upside down with right side facing.

SPECIAL STITCH
Front post treble crochet-single crochet (fptr-sc): Leaving last lp on hook, **fptr** *(see Stitch Guide)* around indicated st. Leaving last lp on hook, sc in st directly behind fptr just made *(3 lps on hook)*, yo, draw lp through 3 lps on hook.

AFGHAN

Row 1 (RS): With A, ch 207, sc in 2nd ch from hook, sc in each of next 4 chs, *3 sc in next ch, sc in each of next 5 chs, sk next 2 chs, sc in each of next 5 chs, rep from * across to last 6 chs, 3 sc in next ch, sc in each of next 5 chs, turn.

Row 2: Ch 1, **sc dec** *(see Stitch Guide)* in first 2 sc, sc in each of next 4 sc, *3 sc in next sc, sc in each of next 5 sc, sk next 2 sc, sc in each of next 5 sc, rep from * across to last 7 sc, 3 sc in next sc, sc in each of next 4 sc, **change color** *(see Pattern Notes)* to B in last st, sc dec in last 2 sc, drop A, **do not fasten off**, turn.

Rows 3 & 4: Rep row 2. At end of row 4, change color to A, drop B, do not fasten off, turn.

Row 5: Ch 1, sc dec in next 2 sc, **fptr-sc** *(see Special Stitch)* around sc directly before 3-sc group 3 rows below, sc in each of next 3 sc on working row, *3 sc in next sc, sc in each of next 3 sc, fptr-sc around each of next 2 sc directly after 3-sc group 3 rows below, sk next 2 sts on working row, fptr-sc around each of next 2 sc directly before 3-sc group 3 rows below, sc in each of next 3 sc on working row, rep from *

across to last 7 sc, 3 sc in next sc, sc in each of next 3 sc, fptr-sc around sc directly after 3-sc group 3 rows below, sc dec in last 2 sc on working row, turn.

Row 6: Rep row 2, change color to B at end of row, drop A, do not fasten off, turn.

Rows 7–158: [Rep rows 3–6 consecutively] 38 times. At end of row 158, fasten off B, do not fasten off A, turn to work down one long side of Afghan.

FIRST SIDE EDGING

Row 1 (WS): With WS of Afghan facing, ch 1, working in ends of rows, sc evenly spaced across long edge of Afghan, turn.

Row 2: Ch 1, sc in each sc across. Fasten off.

2ND SIDE EDGING

Row 1 (WS): With WS of Afghan facing, working in ends of rows on rem long side of Afghan, join A with sl st in end of row, ch 1, sc evenly spaced across long edge of Afghan, turn.

Row 2: Ch 1, sc in each sc across. Fasten off. ■

Bahama Twilight Ripple

SKILL LEVEL

EASY

FINISHED SIZE

44 x 52 inches

MATERIALS

- Caron Simply Soft Collection medium (worsted) weight yarn (6 oz/315 yds/170g per skein):
  5 skeins #0007 aqua mist (*A*)
  4 skeins #0014 pagoda (*B*)
- Size I/9/5.5mm crochet hook or size needed to obtain gauge

GAUGE

7 sc = 2 inches; 11 sc rows = 4 inches

PATTERN NOTES

Weave in loose ends as work progresses.

Change colors (*see Stitch Guide*) in last stitch at end of indicated row.

Carry unused color along edge of work.

When working finishing trim, make sure to work over the unused yarn that has been carried along the side.

SPECIAL STITCH

Front post treble crochet-single crochet (fptr-sc):
Leaving last lp on hook, **fptr** (*see Stitch Guide*) around indicated st. Leaving last lp on hook, sc in st directly behind fptr just made (3 lps on hook), yo, draw lp through 3 lps on hook.

AFGHAN
BODY

Row 1 (RS): With A, ch 203, sc in 2nd ch from hook, sc in each of next 6 chs, *3 sc in next ch, sc in each of next 7 chs, sk next 2 chs, sc in each of next 7 chs, rep from * across to last 8 chs, 3 sc in next ch, sc in each of next 7 chs, turn.

Row 2: Ch 1, **sc dec** *(see Stitch Guide)* in first 2 sc, sc in each of next 6 sc, *3 sc in next sc, sc in each of next 7 sc, sk next 2 sc, sc in each of next 7 sc, rep from * across to last 9 sc, 3 sc in next sc, sc in each of next 6 sc, **change color** *(see Pattern Notes)* to B in last st, sc dec in last 2 sc, drop A, **do not fasten off**, turn.

Rows 3 & 4: Rep row 2. At end of row 4, change color to A, drop B, do not fasten off, turn.

Row 5: Ch 1, sc dec in next 2 sc, sc in each of next 2 sc, continue working across as follows:

a. **fptr-sc** *(see Special Stitch)* around sc directly before 3-sc group 3 rows below, sc in each of next 3 sc on working row;

b. *sc in next sc, fptr-sc around 2nd sc of next 3-sc group 3 rows below, sc in same sc as previous 2 sc on working row;

c. sc in each of next 3 sc, fptr-sc around sc directly after 3-sc group 3 rows below, sc in each of next 3 sc on working row;

d. sk next 2 sc, sc in each of next 3 sc, fptr-sc around sc directly before 3-sc group 3 rows below;

e. sc in each of next 3 sc on working row, rep from * across to last 9 sc;

f. sc in next sc, fptr-sc around 2nd sc of next 3-sc group 3 rows below, sc in same sc as previous 2 sc on working row;

g. sc in each of next 3 sc, fptr-sc around sc directly after 3-sc group 3 rows below, sc in each of next 2 sc, sc dec in last 2 sc, turn.

Row 6: Rep row 2, change color to B at end of row, drop A, do not fasten off, turn.

Rows 7–142: [Rep rows 3–6 consecutively] 34 times. At end of row 142, fasten off B, do not fasten off A, turn to work down long side of afghan.

FIRST SIDE EDGING
Row 1 (WS): With WS of Afghan facing, ch 1, working in ends of rows, sc evenly spaced across long edge of Afghan, turn.

Row 2: Ch 1, sc in each sc across. Fasten off.

2ND SIDE EDGING
Row 1 (WS): With WS of Afghan facing, working in ends of rows on rem long side of Afghan, join A with sl st in end of row, ch 1, sc evenly spaced across long edge of Afghan, turn.

Row 2: Ch 1, sc in each sc across. Fasten off. ∎

Harvest Ripple

Harvest **Ripple**

FINISHED SIZE
52½ x 56¾ inches

MATERIALS
- Caron Simply Soft Collection medium (worsted) weight yarn (6 oz/315 yds/170g per skein):
  3 skeins each #0002 harvest rose *(A)*, #0008 autumn maize *(B)* and #0013 nutmeg *(C)*
- Size I/9/5.5mm crochet hook or size needed to obtain gauge

GAUGE
11 sc = 3¼ inches; 10 sc rows = 4 inches

PATTERN NOTES
Weave in loose ends as work progresses.

Change colors *(see Stitch Guide)* in last stitch at end of indicated row.

Carry unused color along side of work.

When working finishing trim, make sure to work over the unused yarn that has been carried along the side.

SPECIAL STITCH
Front post double crochet-single crochet (fpdc-sc):
Leaving last lp on hook, **fpdc** *(see Stitch Guide)* around indicated st. Leaving last lp on hook, sc in st directly behind fpdc just made *(3 lps on hook)*, yo, draw lp through 3 lps on hook.

AFGHAN
BODY
Row 1: With A, ch 224, sc in 2nd ch from hook, sc in each of next 10 chs, *3 sc in next ch, sc in each of next 11 chs, sk next 2 chs, sc in each of next 11 chs, rep from * across to last 12 chs, 3 sc in next ch, **change color** *(see Pattern Notes)* to B in last sc, sc in each of next 11 chs, drop A, **do not fasten off**, turn.

Row 2 (RS): Ch 1, **sc dec** (*see Stitch Guide*) in first 2 sc, sc in each of next 10 sc, *3 sc in next sc, sc in each of next 11 sc, sk next 2 sc, sc in each of next 11 sc, rep from * across to last 13 sc, 3 sc in next sc, sc in each of next 10 sc, change color to C in last st, sc dec in last 2 sc, drop B, do not fasten off, turn.

Row 3: Rep row 2, change color to A at end of row, drop C, do not fasten off, turn.

Row 4: Ch 1, sc dec in first 2 sc, sc in each of next 2 sc, [**fpdc-sc** (*see Special Stitch*) around next sc 3 rows below, sc in each of next 3 sc on working row] twice, *3 sc in next sc, sc in each of next 3 sc, [fpdc-sc around next sc 3 rows below, sc in each of next 3 sc on working row] twice, sk next 2 sc, sc in each of next 3 sc, [fpdc-sc around next sc 3 rows below, sc in each of next 3 sc on working row] twice, rep from * across to last 13 sc, 3 sc in next sc, [sc in each of next 3 sc, fpdc-sc around next sc 3 rows below] twice, sc in each of next 2 sc on working row, change color to B in last st, sc dec in last 2 sc, drop A, do not fasten off, turn.

Row 5: Rep row 3, change color to C at end of row, drop B, do not fasten off, turn.

Row 6: Rep row 4, change color to A at end of row, drop C, do not fasten off, turn.

Row 7: Rep row 3, change color to B at end of row, drop A, do not fasten off, turn.

Row 8: Rep row 4, change color to C at end of row, drop B, do not fasten off, turn.

Rows 9–140: [Rep rows 3–8 consecutively] 22 times.

Rows 141 & 142: Rep rows 3 and 4. At end of row 142, fasten off B and C, do not fasten off A, turn to work down one long side of Afghan.

FIRST SIDE EDGING
Row 1 (RS): With RS of Afghan facing, ch 1, working in ends of rows, sc evenly sp across long edge of Afghan. Fasten off.

2ND SIDE EDGING
Row 1 (RS): With RS of Afghan facing, working in ends of rows on rem long side of Afghan, join A with sl st in end of first row, ch 1, sc evenly sp across long edge of Afghan. Fasten off. ■

STITCH GUIDE

STITCH ABBREVIATIONS

beg	begin/begins/beginning
bpdc	back post double crochet
bpsc	back post single crochet
bptr	back post treble crochet
CC	contrasting color
ch(s)	chain(s)
ch-	refers to chain or space previously made (i.e., ch-1 space)
ch sp(s)	chain space(s)
cl(s)	cluster(s)
cm	centimeter(s)
dc	double crochet (singular/plural)
dc dec	double crochet 2 or more stitches together, as indicated
dec	decrease/decreases/decreasing
dtr	double treble crochet
ext	extended
fpdc	front post double crochet
fpsc	front post single crochet
fptr	front post treble crochet
g	gram(s)
hdc	half double crochet
hdc dec	half double crochet 2 or more stitches together, as indicated
inc	increase/increases/increasing
lp(s)	loop(s)
MC	main color
mm	millimeter(s)
oz	ounce(s)
pc	popcorn(s)
rem	remain/remains/remaining
rep(s)	repeat(s)
rnd(s)	round(s)
RS	right side
sc	single crochet (singular/plural)
sc dec	single crochet 2 or more stitches together, as indicated
sk	skip/skipped/skipping
sl st(s)	slip stitch(es)
sp(s)	space(s)/spaced
st(s)	stitch(es)
tog	together
tr	treble crochet
trtr	triple treble
WS	wrong side
yd(s)	yard(s)
yo	yarn over

YARN CONVERSION

OUNCES TO GRAMS		GRAMS TO OUNCES	
1	28.4	25	⅞
2	56.7	40	1⅔
3	85.0	50	1¾
4	113.4	100	3½

UNITED STATES		UNITED KINGDOM
sl st (slip stitch)	=	sc (single crochet)
sc (single crochet)	=	dc (double crochet)
hdc (half double crochet)	=	htr (half treble crochet)
dc (double crochet)	=	tr (treble crochet)
tr (treble crochet)	=	dtr (double treble crochet)
dtr (double treble crochet)	=	ttr (triple treble crochet)
skip	=	miss

Reverse Single Crochet (reverse sc): Ch 1. Skip first st. [Working from left to right, insert hook in next st from front to back, draw up lp on hook, yo, and draw through both lps on hook.]

Chain (ch): Yo, pull through lp on hook.

Single crochet (sc): Insert hook in st, yo, pull through st, yo, pull through both lps on hook.

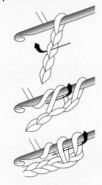

Double crochet (dc): Yo, insert hook in st, yo, pull through st, [yo, pull through 2 lps] twice.

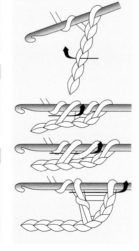

Front loop (front lp) Back loop (back lp)

Front Loop   Back Loop

Front post stitch (fp): Back post stitch (bp): When working post st, insert hook from right to left around post st on previous row.

Back   Front

Post of Stitch

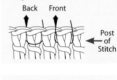

Half double crochet (hdc): Yo, insert hook in st, yo, pull through st, yo, pull through all 3 lps on hook.

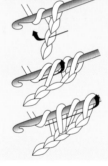

Double treble crochet (dtr): Yo 3 times, insert hook in st, yo, pull through st, [yo, pull through 2 lps] 4 times.

Slip stitch (sl st): Insert hook in st, pull through both lps on hook.

Chain Color Change (ch color change) Yo with new color, draw through last lp on hook.

Double Crochet Color Change (dc color change) Drop first color, yo with new color, draw through last 2 lps of st.

Treble crochet (tr): Yo twice, insert hook in st, yo, pull through st, [yo, pull through 2 lps] 3 times.

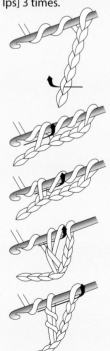

Single crochet decrease (sc dec): (Insert hook, yo, draw lp through) in each of the sts indicated, yo, draw through all lps on hook.

Example of 2-sc dec

Half double crochet decrease (hdc dec): (Yo, insert hook, yo, draw lp through) in each of the sts indicated, yo, draw through all lps on hook.

Example of 2-hdc dec

Double crochet decrease (dc dec): (Yo, insert hook, yo, draw loop through, draw through 2 lps on hook) in each of the sts indicated, yo, draw through all lps on hook.

Example of 2-dc dec

Treble crochet decrease (tr dec): Holding back last lp of each st, tr in each of the sts indicated, yo, pull through all lps on hook.

Example of 2-tr dec

Metric Conversion Charts

METRIC CONVERSIONS

yards	x	.9144	=	metres (m)
yards	x	91.44	=	centimetres (cm)
inches	x	2.54	=	centimetres (cm)
inches	x	25.40	=	millimetres (mm)
inches	x	.0254	=	metres (m)

centimetres	x	.3937	=	inches
metres	x	1.0936	=	yards

INCHES INTO MILLIMETRES & CENTIMETRES (Rounded off slightly)

inches	mm	cm	inches	cm	inches	cm	inches	cm
1/8	3	0.3	5	12.5	21	53.5	38	96.5
1/4	6	0.6	5 1/2	14	22	56	39	99
3/8	10	1	6	15	23	58.5	40	101.5
1/2	13	1.3	7	18	24	61	41	104
5/8	15	1.5	8	20.5	25	63.5	42	106.5
3/4	20	2	9	23	26	66	43	109
7/8	22	2.2	10	25.5	27	68.5	44	112
1	25	2.5	11	28	28	71	45	114.5
1 1/4	32	3.2	12	30.5	29	73.5	46	117
1 1/2	38	3.8	13	33	30	76	47	119.5
1 3/4	45	4.5	14	35.5	31	79	48	122
2	50	5	15	38	32	81.5	49	124.5
2 1/2	65	6.5	16	40.5	33	84	50	127
3	75	7.5	17	43	34	86.5		
3 1/2	90	9	18	46	35	89		
4	100	10	19	48.5	36	91.5		
4 1/2	115	11.5	20	51	37	94		

KNITTING NEEDLES CONVERSION CHART

Canada/U.S.	0	1	2	3	4	5	6	7	8	9	10	10½	11	13	15
Metric (mm)	2	2¼	2¾	3¼	3½	3¾	4	4½	5	5½	6	6½	8	9	10

CROCHET HOOKS CONVERSION CHART

Canada/U.S.	1/B	2/C	3/D	4/E	5/F	6/G	8/H	9/I	10/J	10½/K	N
Metric (mm)	2.25	2.75	3.25	3.5	3.75	4.25	5	5.5	6	6.5	9.0

RETAIL STORES: If you would like to carry this pattern book or any other DRG publications, visit DRGwholesale.com

Every effort has been made to ensure that the instructions in this publication are complete and accurate. We cannot, however, take responsibility for human error, typographical mistakes or variations in individual work. Please visit AnniesCustomerCare.com to check for pattern updates.

ISBN: 978-1-59635-356-5

1 2 3 4 5 6 7 8 9